Papua New Guinea's Origins

SOCIAL SCIENCE PUPIL BOOK

AF583769

Department of Education
Papua New Guinea

© 1988 Department of Education, Papua New Guinea
First Published 1988
Reprinted 1990, 1993, 1994, 1995, 1996 (twice), 1997, 1999 (three times), 2000 (twice), 2002, 2007, 2008 (twice), 2015 (D)

All rights reserved. No part of this publication may be reproduced, stored in a retrieval system, or transmitted, in any form or by any means, electronic, mechanical, photocopying, recording or otherwise, without the prior written permission of the publisher.
ISBN 9980 58208 1
ISBN 978 9980 58208 9
National Library of Papua New Guinea

Cover Photograph by courtesy of the Photo Office of Tourism, Boroko

Written by Kate Halstead, with editorial assistance from Brian Deutrom
Designed by Steve Randles
Typeset by Abb Typesetting Pty Ltd, Collingwood, Victoria, Australia
Printed in Australia by Ligare Pty Ltd
Published by Department of Education, Papua New Guinea
Prepared by Oxford University Press
253 Normanby Road, South Melbourne, Australia

Acknowledgements

The Papua New Guinea Department of Education acknowledges the contribution of many individuals at the Curriculum Unit, the University of Papua New Guinea, the National Museum, and on the Social Science Syllabus Advisory Committee to the trialling and review of the book. The participation of the teachers and students at the trial schools—Kilakila, Badihagwa, Laloki, Gerehu, and Tusbab—is greatly appreciated.

The authors and publishers wish to thank copyright holders for supplying, and granting permission to reproduce, the following photographs, drawings, maps and articles:

Academic Press, Sydney, Australia (from J. Peter White & James F. O'Connell, *A Prehistory of Australia, New Guinea, and Sahul*, 1982, p. 188; original source unknown), p. 40 (top);

The Bettmann Archive, New York, U.S.A., p. 13 (lower right);

Bruce French & Celia Bridle, *Food Crops of Papua New Guinea*, Vudal College of Agriculture, East New Britain (pp. 13, 16, 17, 25, 29, 31, 41, 43), p. 21;

GASPP, Elwood, Vic., Australia, p. 11;

Professor L. Groube, University of Papua New Guinea, pp. 25 (top), 29 (middle);

Mountford-Sheard Collection, State Library of South Australia, Adelaide, Australia, p. 13 (top right) (Pitjandjara woman carrying wooden dish);

National Museum of Papua New Guinea, pp. 12 (lower), 14 (nos 1, 6), 22 (lower left), 30 (top and centre), 31 (top and centre), 32 (lower), 37 (top), 38 (top), 45 (top right), 46 (lower left), 47 (lower right);

New Scientist, 25 Dec. 1986–1 Jan. 1987, p. 52;

Papua New Guinea Archives, Department of Education, pp. 7 (top left and right), 13 (lower left), 22 (lower right), 23, 24 (top right), 33, 36 (top and centre), 39 (top), 44 (top), 45 (top left), 46 (lower right), 47 (top left), 48 (lower);

Illustrations first published in P. Ryan (gen. ed.), *Encyclopaedia of Papua New Guinea*, Melbourne University Press, Carlton, Vic., Australia, in association with the University of Papua New Guinea, 1972, vol. 1, p. 425; vol. 2, pp. 717, 718, 963, 965, 968), pp. 12 (top), 14 (nos 2–5, 7–8);

Reed Methuen Publishers Ltd, Wellington, New Zealand (adaptations from Graeme R. Stevens, *New Zealand Adrift*, A. H. & A. W. Reed, Wellington, 1981, pp. 42, 291, 292), pp. 16 (lower), 17 (top left and right);

Science Museum of Victoria, Melbourne, Australia, p. 10.

Disclaimer: Every effort has been made to trace the original source of copyright material in this book. The publishers would be pleased to hear from copyright holders to rectify any errors or omissions.

Secretary's Message

The topic **Papua New Guinea's Origins** is the first term's work in the Grade Eight Provincial High School Social Science Course. It is the second of the four topics which develop the theme **Change** through Grades Seven to Ten.

The book is the core learning material for the topic. A supporting set of teaching notes is available. The teaching notes advise the teachers on how to make the best use of the pupil's book.

The material in the book integrates the presentation of information, the development of ideas, reinforcement and application of Social Science skills and the fostering of attitudes.

Three types of activities appear at the end of each section. There are *Exercises* to ensure comprehension of the material; there are *Things to discuss* and *Things to do*. The activities combine work on sections of the book with direct investigations both inside and outside school.

J. E. Tetaga
Secretary for Education

This book is one of the items of instructional material produced for Provincial High Schools in Papua New Guinea as part of the Education III Textbook Sub-Project.

Contents

Introduction

Let us take you on a journey through time. It is a story about our **origins**. The word "origins" means starting point. In order for us to learn about the origins of Papua New Guinea we have to understand the origins of the Earth itself. This is a *very* long story.

There are many questions about our origins which remain unanswered. The story of our origins is like a time jigsaw puzzle. We are finding new information every day, and understanding more of the puzzle. There are many topics in this book that you may like to study in more detail. Find some books on these topics in your school library.

This book is also about **change**. As we go through time, we can see that our world has constantly changed; it is still changing today, and will continue to change tomorrow. The way we live now has been influenced by our past. If we can understand some of the past events that have made us what we are, perhaps it will help us to plan a better future. Our world is very precious. Like all living things it needs care and understanding.

In chapters 1 and 2 you will read about the *origins* of the earth. Chapters 3 and 4 cover the origins of the *land* we call Papua New Guinea, and chapters 5 to 7 the origins of the *people* of Papua New Guinea.

1. How Did the Earth Begin?

People have always asked the question, "How did the Earth begin?" Many societies throughout the world have their own stories of how the earth began.

One story comes from the Orokolo people, in the Gulf Province of Papua New Guinea, and is from a story called *Orokolo Genesis*, by Morea Pekoro:

In the beginning there was no land, mountains, or people. The surface of the world was covered with water. Only one thing lived: a giant turtle which swam slowly around until, wishing to rest, it used its powerful flippers to scrape and push up land from the bottom of the sea. After much scraping, the first land to rise above the surface of the water appeared. This land was bright and shiny because it contained the life that was later to come out of it. It was hot too, and the new land shone and sparkled as the waves rolled onto it. At night-time it twinkled like fireflies.

This land grew and grew, until at last the turtle climbed onto it and rested. When he had finished resting, he dug holes in the ground, each bigger than a human house, and laid eggs in them. He travelled some distance away, dug more holes, and laid more eggs.

After a while some of the eggs hatched, and the first humans came out. The very first people were Ivi Apo and Kerema Apo. These were the first ancestors of Man. They looked at each other, and Kerema Apo said, "I am Kerema Apo and this is my land. It is a beautiful land, and will produce many things".

As the turtle's other eggs hatched, many different kinds of trees and vegetables appeared from the eggs. These grew till they covered the land. The place where the plants appeared was the first land in the world, and today this place is still called Kerema.

The next story comes from the ancient Jewish people, and is now the Christians' story of how the Earth began. It is from the first chapter of the Bible:

In the beginning God created the Heavens and the Earth. The Earth was without form, and empty, and darkness was on the face of the deep. On the first day, God said, "Let there be light", and there was light. On the second day, God said, "Let there be Heaven".

On the third day, God said, "Let the waters under Heaven gather together in one place and let the dry land appear also". In this way, the seas and the land were made; and God saw that they too were good. Then He said, "Let the Earth bring forth all green things and let fruit grow on the trees. Every plant shall bear fruit".

On the fourth day, God said, "Let there be lights in Heaven, so that Day shall be divided from Night. These lights shall show the changing of the seasons, and the passing of the years", and He made the Sun, the Moon, and the stars.

On the fifth day, He said, "Let the seas bring forth all fish and water creatures, and let birds fly in the sky; and may they flourish and multiply".

On the sixth day, God said, "Let the Earth bring forth every kind of living creature and living thing, and may they cover the Earth with their kind". Then He said, "Let us make Men in our image, and let them rule over all other creatures that have been made". So God made Mankind, both male and female, and he blessed them. Then he looked and saw the multitude of creatures, and He saw that it was good.

On the seventh day, God rested, after His works of creation.

The movement of the continents is felt today as **earthquakes** and **volcanic eruptions**. Liquid rock escapes to the surface during these eruptions.

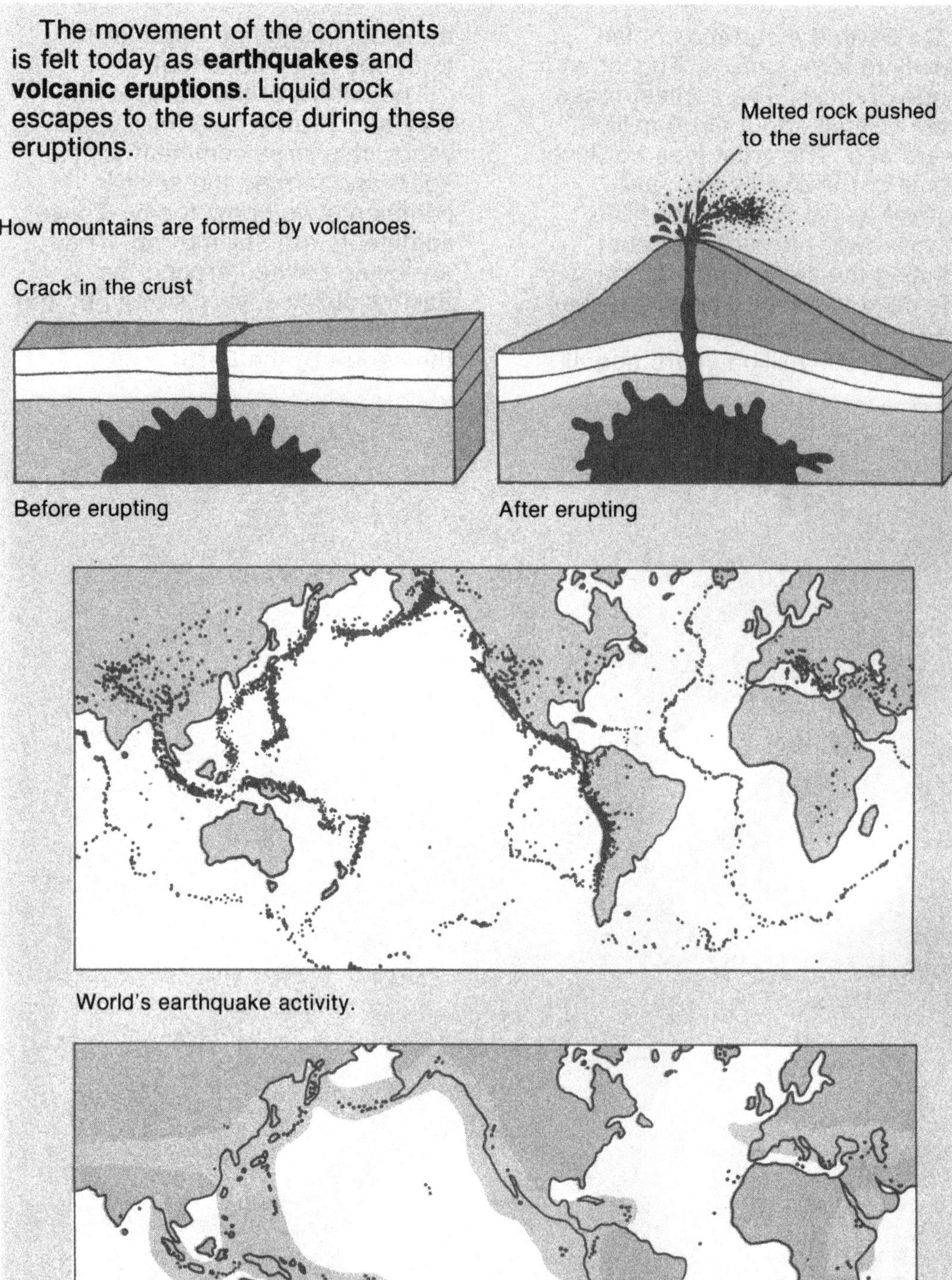

World's earthquake activity.

Volcanic region
· Each dot represents an active volcano

World's volcanic activity.

A volcano in Papua New Guinea.

After an earthquake in Papua New Guinea.

Life did not develop on the Earth for a long time, and first appeared in the seas. Scientists think that the simplest of water plants developed about 1500 million years ago. About 500 million years ago many types of jellyfish, sponges and worms lived in the seas of the Earth. The first fish appeared about 400 million years ago. About 350 million years ago life moved on to the land.

Man seems to have lived on the Earth for the last two million years. The earliest evidence we have of true Man comes from the African continent. Man is very new on the planet Earth.

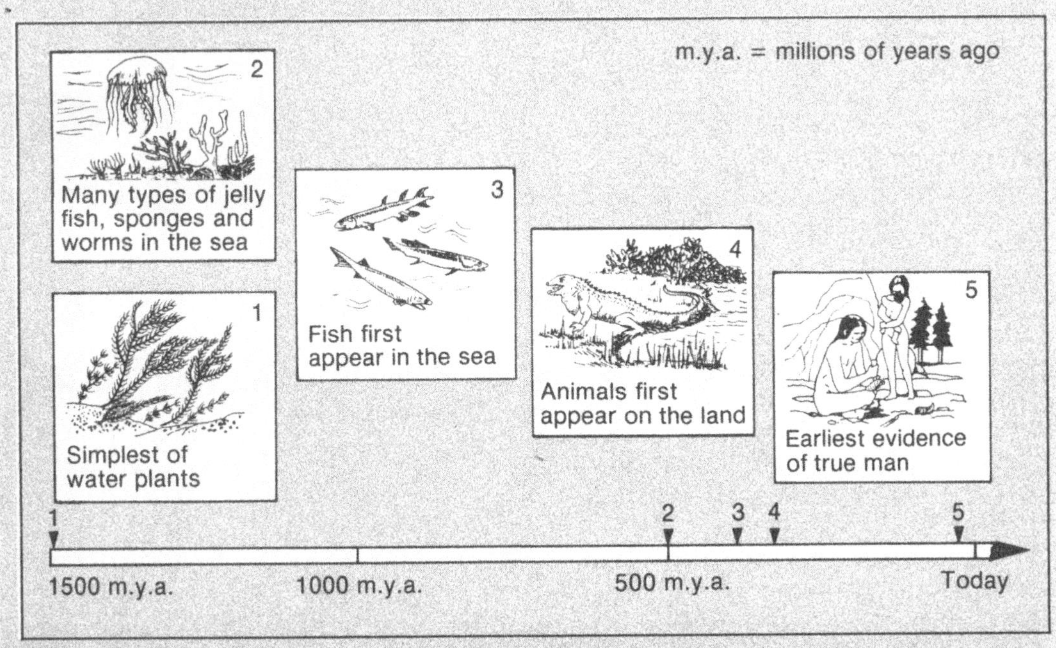

Time-line to show the development of life on earth.

It is very difficult for us to think about such enormous periods of time. If the story of the Earth was written in a 1000-page book, man would not appear until the last page. The earliest evidence of Man in the land we now call Papua New Guinea is about 50 000 years old.

The four stories about how the Earth began differ in detail, but they all express similar ideas. There is one difference between the science story and the other stories. The science story changes as time goes by. It changes as more information is found. Scientists are inquisitive people, and they try to find out more about how things work.

Activities

Exercises

1. What is the meaning of the word "**origins**"?
2. Write one sentence from each of the following stories which explains what it was like before the Earth was made:
   - Orokolo Genesis,
   - Bible story,
   - Chinese story.
3. The scientists' story.
   Did you understand:
   (a) What is the solar system?
   (b) How the Earth was formed?
   (c) When the Earth was formed?
   (d) Can you write these sentences in the correct order?
   - The Sun began to form at the centre of this cloud.
   - The Earth and the other planets were formed later.
   - The Solar System began as a huge cloud of dust and gas.

   (e) How the water was formed?
   (f) How long ago all the land was joined together?
   (g) Why did the land start to split apart?
   (h) How do we know the continents are still moving?
   (i) What do you notice about the distribution of the world's earthquakes and volcanoes?

Things to discuss

In groups discuss the similarities between the first three creation stories. Discuss any creation stories you know from your village.

Things to do

1. Go to your library and find out more about how the Earth was formed. If you look at several different books about the Earth and its development you may notice that different books give slightly different dates for when things happened. Why do you think this is? (Read the second paragraph in the introduction on page 1 to help you answer this question.)
2. A time-line is a type of calendar on which important dates and events have been recorded. Copy the time-line on page 7 into your exercise book. Explain what is meant by the sentence, "Man is very new on the planet Earth".
3. Make a table comparing the sequence of events for the development of life on Earth in the Bible story and the scientists' story. What do you notice about the two stories?
4. Prepare a time-line to show the important events in your life from the time you were born up to the present.
5. What is one difference between the scientists' story and the other stories?

2. How Do We Know?

You may well be asked how scientists learn things about our world. In Grade 7 you learned that the study of the past is called history, and that historians use written and spoken records to discover things about the past.

The time before things were written down is called **prehistory**. Scientists have had no written records to tell them about how the Earth was formed or how life developed on Earth. They have used clues, like detectives, to help them develop explanations of things that happened in the past. Many different kinds of scientists have helped to build the story of how the Earth was formed.

Some scientists study the stars. Their information has helped to develop the story of how the sun and the solar system were formed.

Some scientists study rocks. They have found clues that have helped us to understand the history of the Earth.

Other scientists study living things and their remains. They study the remains of plants and animals that are sometimes found inside rocks. These remains may be plants, the bones or shells of animals or even whole animals, that have been trapped in soil that later changed into rocks. These remains are called **fossils**. By working out the age of the rocks in which fossils are found, scientists can tell us when the animals or plants lived on Earth. All the evidence we have about the development of living things on Earth comes from fossils.

These leaves were growing millions of years ago in a tropical forest. You can even see their veins.

This is a fossil shellfish.

Scientists who study the development of Man from the things men have made and used are called **archaeologists**. They search for clues in places where our **ancestors** lived and worked. Caves, cooking fires, gardens and burial places are all important sites for archaeologists.

People living in caves.

Archaeologists look for objects that were made or used by Man. The ashes from their fires, the animal bones and shells from their meals, their tools and weapons, their household rubbish, and of course their own bones, give archaeologists valuable clues. Archaeologists look for these **artefacts** by digging in the ground. They brush the earth away very gently, taking care not to break anything they find. Like all scientists, they keep careful records of everything they discover.

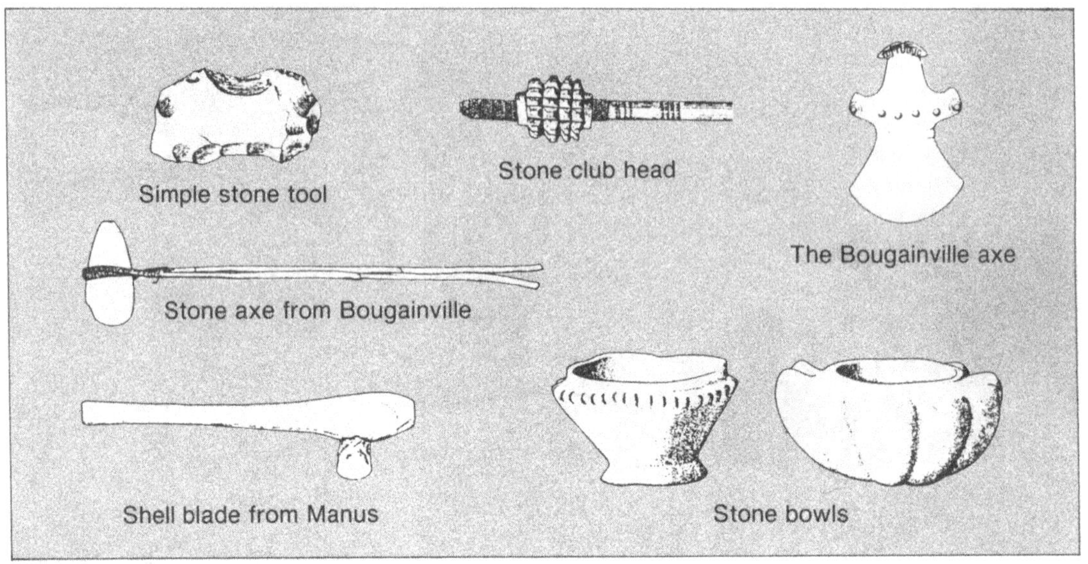

Artefacts from Papua New Guinea.

Archaeologists working in Papua New Guinea.

Most of the things that early man used have disappeared by now. Only the most hard-wearing materials have survived.

In recent years some scientists have developed a way of measuring the age of materials which contain carbon. The remains of all plants and animals contain carbon. This method is called **radiocarbon dating**, and it is very helpful to archaeologists. Scientists are now trying to improve this method of dating so that objects can be dated back at least as far as 70 000 years ago.

Other scientists, called **linguists**, study the languages spoken by different people. They are able to work out the relationships between different languages. These relationships show the *connections between the people who* speak the languages.

In some parts of the world there are people living just as their ancestors did thousands of years ago. Papua New Guinea is one of the few areas in the world in which many people still live in the traditional life-style.

Historic photograph of Papua New Guinean village scene.

Much knowledge about the past has been gained by observing traditional life-styles.

Traditional Aboriginal at work.

Traditional Amazon Indian.

By studying all the information that has been found out about our Earth and its people we can begin to understand about its beginning.

Activities

Exercises

1. What does "prehistory" mean?
2. Why do we say that scientists are like detectives?
3. Here are the names of three different types of scientists; **geologists**, **astronomers**, **biologists**. Write the following sentences in your exercise book. Use a dictionary to help you write the correct name of the type of scientist next to each sentence.
   - Some scientists study the stars.
   - Some scientists study rocks.
   - Other scientists study living things and their remains.
4. What are fossils?
5. What do archaeologists do?
6. Why have most artefacts used by early Man disappeared?
7. How has radio-carbon dating helped the archaeologist?

Things to discuss

In groups, discuss why it is important for people not to forget about their traditional life-styles.

Things to do

1. Make a list of all the places where archaeologists go to look for evidence of early Man.
2. Go to your library and find out more about the work of archaeologists.
3. Write a few sentences explaining how we have found out about our prehistory.
4. This picture shows a number of artefacts which have been dug up from a site in Papua New Guinea. Use the labels provided to name each artefact.

   What do these artefacts tell you about the village where they were found?

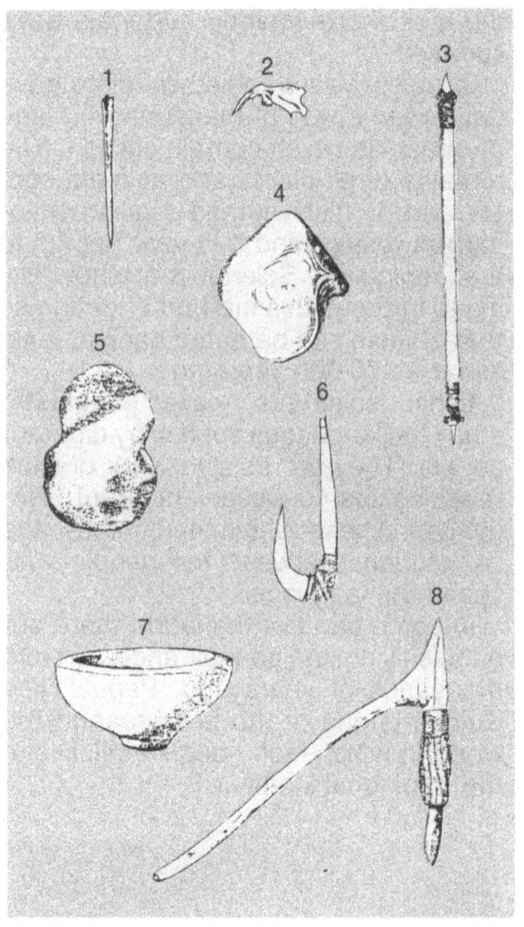

Shark's tooth tool
Used for carving designs on shells and other hard surfaces.

Adze
A tool with a sharpened stone tied onto the handle. Used for digging the soil.

Needle
This tool has been made from bone.

Shell
Used for peeling vegetables.

Small carving tool
Made from the jaw of a small marsupial.

Fish hook
This tool has been made from bone.

Stone axe
This large stone axe used to be tied onto a handle.

Stone mortar
A stone dish.

5. You are going to be an archaeologist for a day. Select a place where the school used to dump or burn rubbish. Find yourself some digging tools.

   Mark out an area of one square metre in which you will dig. First look at the surface of your area and record what you find. Now dig down carefully in layers of about 10 cm, and record what you find in each layer. Record both the location and the name of the objects that you find, e.g.

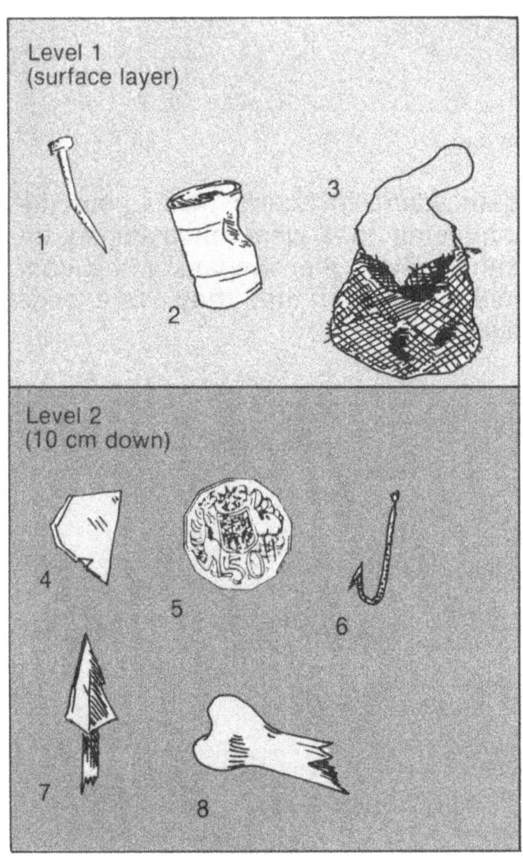

Record of artefacts

1. Rusty nail.	**5.** Australian 50 cent coin.
2. Oil tin.	**6.** Rusty fish hook.
3. Old bag.	**7.** Old arrow head.
4. Broken glass.	**8.** Piece of broken bone.

   Draw a sketch map to show the location of your site. Write a few sentences explaining what you have found.

6. Make a picture poster to show some traditional ways of living in your village.

3. The Land of Papua New Guinea

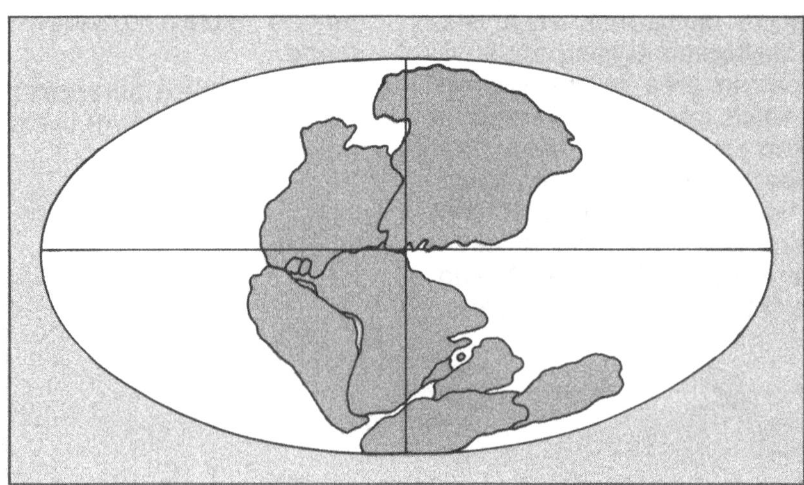

The Earth may have looked like this 200 million years ago.

We begin the story of **our** origins by learning about the formation of the land itself. Scientists have been able to find out a great deal about the development of our earth. They believe that the land was once one huge continent. They think that this continent slowly broke apart because of intense heat from the centre of the Earth.

These huge continents continued to split apart, and formed the smaller continents that we know today. Scientists have evidence to support the existence of these huge continents. They have found identical fossils throughout the continents that were once joined together. Even the shapes of the continents suggest that they were once joined.

Key

+ Fossil plants

Fossil and living birds

Fossil reptile

Fossil and living trees

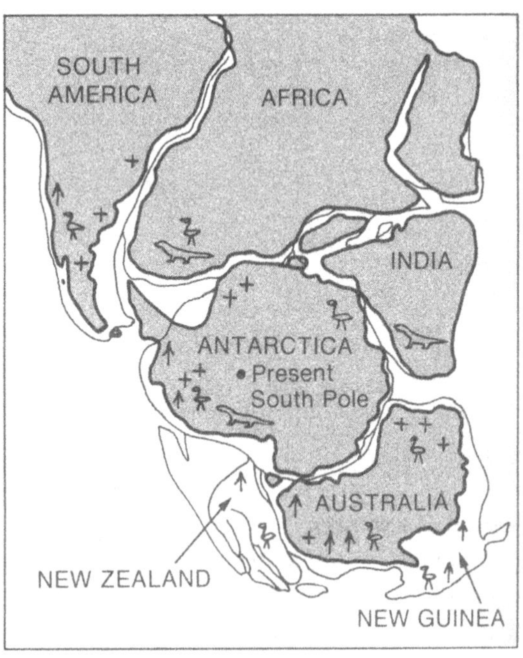

Map showing fossils that have been found throughout continents that were once joined.

The land we call New Guinea was formed from part of the early Australian continent. The land we call Australia was formed when the huge continent started to split up. About 100 million years ago the Australian continent slowly started moving northwards. As this happened the Australian continent pressed against the land mass to the north of it. This pressure forced the first mountain peaks of New Guinea above the surface of the ocean. This happened about 25 million years ago. Today we still find fossil shellfish and fishbones at the top of some of the highest mountains in Papua New Guinea.

About 13 million years ago the land of New Guinea began to get the shape that it has today.

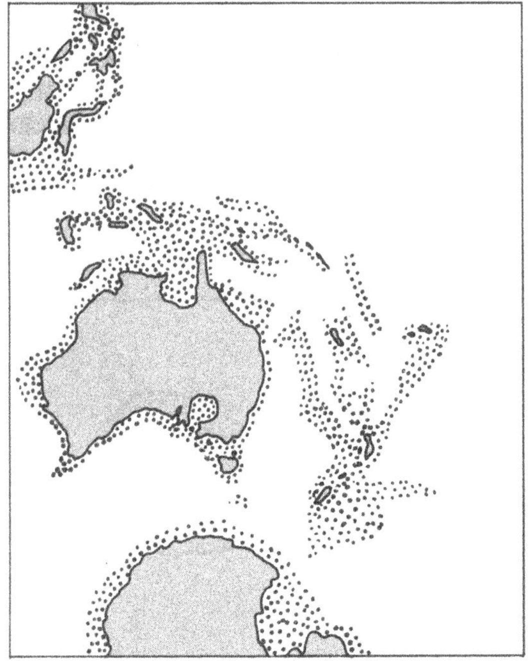

25 million years ago the first mountain peaks of New Guinea appeared above the sea.

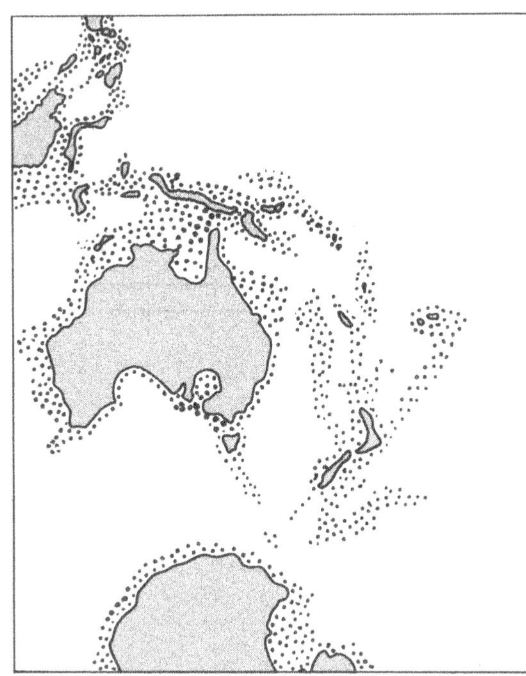

About 13 million years ago the land of New Guinea began to get the shape that it has today.

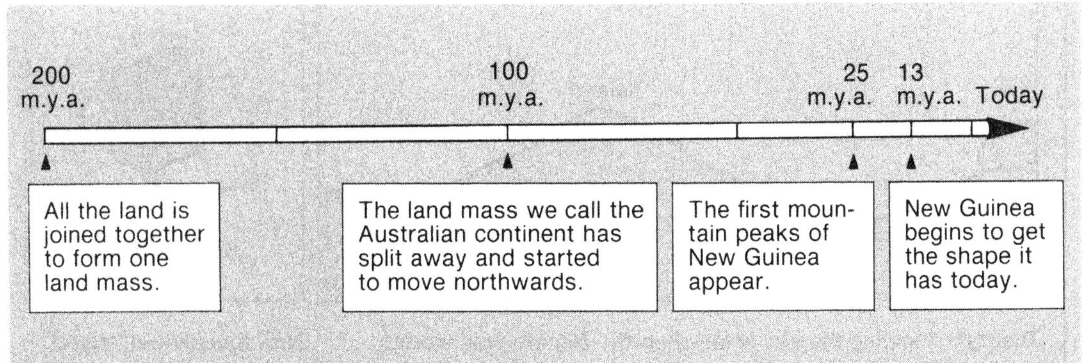

Time-line showing the development of the land of New Guinea.

6. Food

About 18 000 years ago the Earth's climate started to change and become warmer. People were able to live in places which were too cold before. Very slowly people began to move into these higher mountain areas.

Scientists now believe that people had settled in the whole of the Highlands of Papua New Guinea by 10 000 years ago. These people slowly changed their way of life from hunting and collecting food to a more settled life-style. They cleared forest land, planted their own food plants, and started gardens.

Archaeologists believe that some of the oldest evidence of gardening on Earth has been found in Papua New Guinea. The development of gardens meant that, instead of moving around from place to place searching for food, people were able to stay in one place. Instead of living in simple rock shelters and caves they began to build houses for themselves. It was the start of village life. The remains of a house found recently in the Eastern Highlands may be the oldest remains of a house in the world.

When our ancestors first discovered that they could grow their own food it was one of the most important discoveries of the human race. Papua New Guinea is now thought to be one of the many birthplaces of garden agriculture.

A cleared garden site.

Today much of the land that was forest, and was cleared for gardens, has now become grassland. The trees probably did not regrow because of the continual burning of the land by our ancestors. They may have burned the land to make gardening and hunting easier.

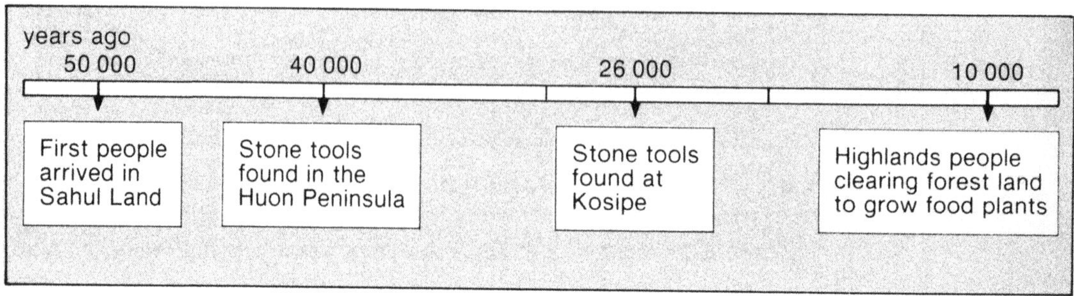

In the last chapter you read about the famous stone axes of Kosipe in the central highlands of the Central Province. The presence of Man at Kosipe about 26 000 years ago has been confirmed by another discovery. A nearby swamp has been excavated and fossils of **pollen** grains have been found. Scientists have shown that the pollen grains are from different types of grasses. These grasses were growing because people had cleared the forest.

The size and shape of some of the Kosipe axes make archaeologists think that they were not hunting tools. Perhaps they were being used for early gardening techniques to encourage certain food plants to grow better at the forest edge. Evidence from elsewhere in the world shows that man did not begin garden agriculture until 10 000 years ago. If people were using gardening tools at Kosipe 26 000 years ago, Papua New Guinea could indeed be one of the birthplaces of agriculture. The evidence of the stone axes on the Huon Peninsula provides more support for this theory. However, we still need more evidence before we can be sure.

As well as the stone tools and fossil evidence, archaeologists have discovered other evidence about the development of agriculture in Papua New Guinea. Some of the most exciting evidence comes from Kuk, a plantation 7 kilometres from the town of Mt Hagen in the Western Highlands Province. Archaeologists have found what appear to be drainage ditches, which date back 9000 years.

Date:	9000 years ago.
Place:	Kuk plantation, Western Highlands Province.
Evidence:	Remains of organic materials in man-made drainage ditches.
Importance:	Land used for growing food; ditches draining land.

It is in the sides of the new drains of the Kuk tea plantation that the prehistoric ditches have been found.

These prehistoric ditches are obviously man-made. Why were they built? There must be a good reason, because it involved a lot of hard work.

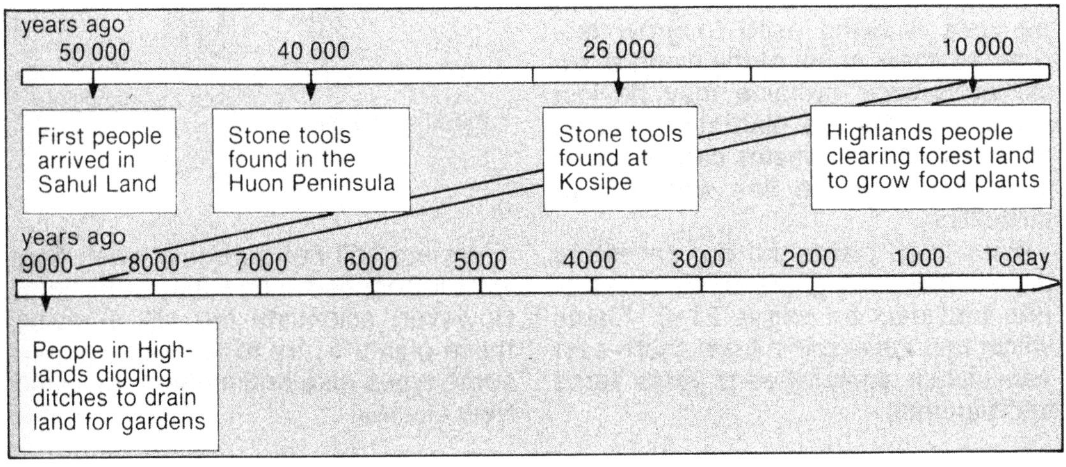

The filled-in prehistoric ditches can be seen in the grey clay.

Archaeologists think these ditches show that this area was being used to grow food from as early as 9000 years ago. Perhaps the people were growing local bananas and yams, or possibly a type of taro which may have originated in Papua New Guinea.

Scientists believe that agricultural ditches were used in this area until about 1250 years ago. The area then seems to have been abandoned. They think the sweet potato appeared in the area about 300 to 400 years ago. Today the area is being used to grow tea. Unfortunately, some of the world's oldest agricultural remains may be lost because of the tea plantation. Let us hope part of the remains can be saved as a tribute to the fine work of our ancestors.

What food plants did our ancestors grow in their early gardens? See the picture and map on pages 21–2. Plants which may have come from south-east Asia include some types of yams, taros and bananas.

We are still not sure just when they were introduced or how they came here. However, scientists are still studying these plants to try to find out whether some types also originated from island New Guinea.

The Sweet Potato

The sweet potato deserves a special mention because it is such an important food crop in Papua New Guinea.

Date:	400 years ago.
Place:	Highlands region.
Evidence:	Sweet potato.
Importance:	It slowly replaced taro as the main food crop in the highlands.

The sweet potato originates from South and Central America. Until recently it was thought that the Portuguese and Spanish brought the sweet potato to Papua New Guinea about 300 to 400 years ago from south-east Asia. We know that the Portuguese took it to Portugal from Central America about 500 years ago. However, it may have come by another route. Archaeological discoveries in New Zealand and Hawaii suggest that the sweet potato grew in Polynesia over a thousand years ago. It is therefore possible that the sweet potato could have reached Papua New Guinea from the east earlier than 400 years ago. We need more evidence before we can be sure.

The sweet potato adapted well to the Highlands environment, and proved an easy crop to grow. It grew better at higher altitudes than other crops, and also produced a bigger yield. The sweet potato needs the same gardening techniques as other root crops, and the technology required to grow it was already well known to the Papua New Guinean gardeners.

Sweet potato gardens.

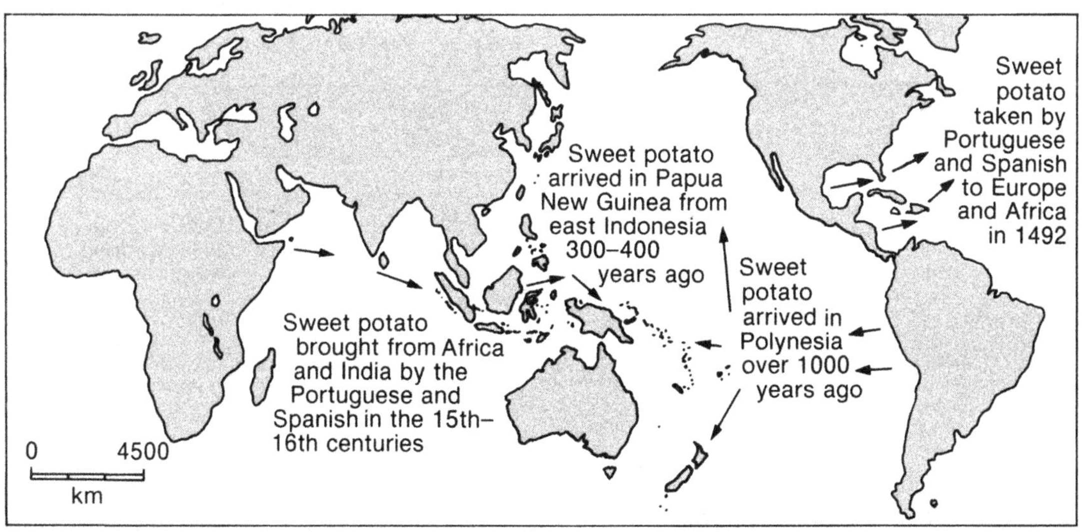

Map of the world showing how the sweet potato arrived in our region.

The Pig

Another newcomer to Papua New Guinea is the pig. There is definite evidence of pigs in Papua New Guinea for the last 6000 years and less evidence for the last 10 000 years.

Date:	10 000 (?) years ago.
Place:	Niobe rock shelter, Eastern Highlands Province; Yuku rock shelter, Western Highlands Province.
Evidence:	Pigs' teeth found in soil which dates back 10 000 years. One of the teeth may be 10 000 years old.
Importance:	May be the first signs of pigs.

Date:	6000 years ago.
Place:	Many rock shelters.
Evidence:	Pigs' bones.
Importance:	Definite evidence of pigs.

The evidence is very confusing. Pigs are definitely not native to island New Guinea. They arrived here from somewhere else. Where did they come from? Did they swim from Sunda Land? The great scientist Alfred Wallace reported seeing them swimming across the Straits of Molucca in 1869! Were they transported here by man? Pig bones have only been found together with evidence of Man, so we think that Man was responsible for the introduction of pigs to Papua New Guinea.

How long have pigs been here, and where did they come from? Did they arrive by the same method and at the same time as the Asian plants? For now, all we can say is that we are not sure.

There is also confusion about the arrival of the pig in Australia. There is no evidence to show that there were pigs in Australia before the arrival of the Europeans 200 years ago. This is very strange. If pigs have been in Papua New Guinea for at least 10 000 years, then why did they not reach Australia? After all, it was possible to walk between Papua New Guinea and Australia until about 7000 years ago.

The number of pig bones found at the archaeological sites increases as we move towards the present time, particularly over the last 1000 years. What caused this increase? Was it just the natural reproductive cycle, or were the pigs being looked after and fed by people, and therefore increasing more rapidly? Could the arrival of the sweet potato have anything to do with the increase? For the moment, all we can say is "We're not sure".

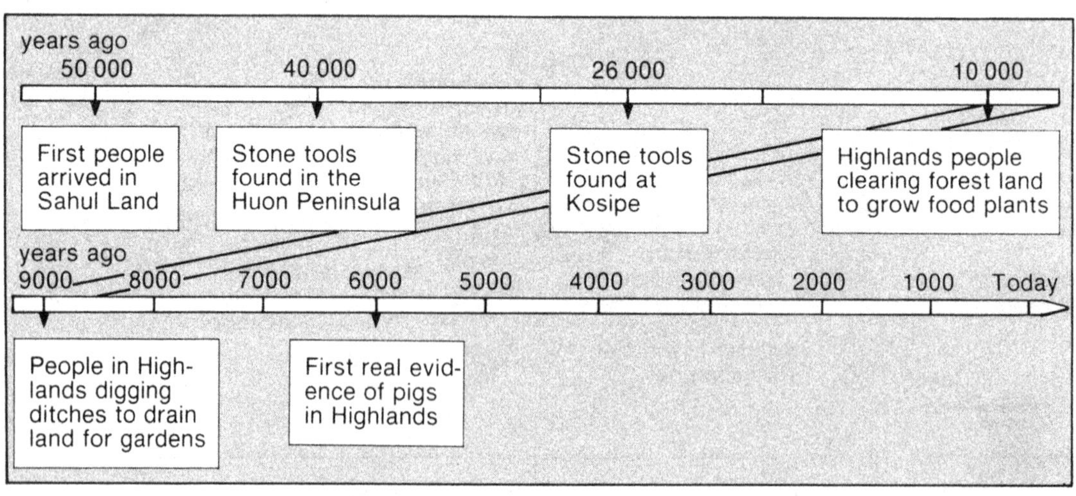

Pigs being hunted while swimming.

Man's Impact on the Land

Since Man first arrived in Sahul Land he has used the land to provide him with all his needs. Man has always made use of the forest to supply these needs. It has provided him with his food, water, medicines, and the materials needed to build houses and shelters, canoes and rafts, tools and weapons, clothing and containers.

For a long time the effect of Man on his land was not great, but when he started making gardens he started to clear the forest from his land. As the population increased he needed to make more gardens in order to grow more food. More of the forests started to disappear. Much of the good soil was lost, and grasslands appeared where forests used to be.

Today the forest is under much greater threat. Large areas of land have been taken over by timber companies, and many more areas have now been cleared. Wild plants, birds and animals have been lost in the process. In many places, only those people living close to areas of uncleared forest continue to hunt regularly. Wallabies are not found today in most of the man-made grassland areas of the Highland valleys. These animals prefer forest or forest-edge environments. Some animals have become very rare because of hunting. The long-beaked echidna no longer survives on the eastern slopes of Mt Wilhelm, though it was hunted there in living memory.

We must plan for our future carefully if we want our land to continue providing us with the things we need.

Activities

Exercises

1. Why do you think people started clearing away forest land? What has happened to much of this land today?
2. What do archaeologists think the Kosipe stone tools were used for?
3. What have we found out from the prehistoric ditches found on the Kuk tea plantation?
4. Why is it important for us to not destroy these ditches?
5. What is the main difference between the Pacific banana and the Asian banana?
6. Why did the sweet potato replace taro as the main food crop in the Highlands?
7. The sweet potato originates from South America. From which two directions could it have arrived in Papua New Guinea?
8. Why do we think that pigs were introduced by Man into island New Guinea?
9. What effect has the sweet potato had on the pig population of Papua New Guinea?

Things to discuss

1. In groups discuss the evidence to support the sentence, "Papua New Guinea could indeed be one of the birthplaces of agriculture".
2. In groups discuss the sentence, "We must plan for our future very carefully if we want our land to continue providing us with the things we need".

Things to do

1. Here is a list showing the possible stages in the development of gardening in Papua New Guinea:
   (a) hunting and collecting food from the forest;
   (b) encouraging certain plants to grow at the forest edge;
   (c) having permanent sites at the forest edge where selected plants are grown;
   (d) having permanent fenced sites for growing selected food plants.

   Write these four stages in your exercise book.
2. Now read the following information. Archaeologists who have studied the stone axes from the Huon Peninsula have come to the following conclusions:
   (a) The tools were used not just for working the soil.
   Evidence: Soil working tends to "polish" stone tools. There is little evidence of this.
   (b) The tools were not used for cutting down big trees.
   Evidence: The cutting edge is not strong enough.
   (c) The tools were used for hitting hard surfaces, such as the branches and roots of trees and plants.
   Evidence: The way in which a large number of the tools are broken suggests that the axes, despite their weak cutting edge, often hit hard material.

   From the evidence presented, which stage of development in question 1, above, would make most use of the stone axes. Give reasons for your findings.

   Why do you think people started putting fences around their gardens? Why do people still do this today?
3. Copy these paragraphs into your exercise book:

> If you ever find any artefacts that may be of interest to historians, please write to the National Museum. We need

these artefacts to give us information about the way we lived in the past.

It is against the law for people to touch places such as old village sites and burial grounds.

Why do you think we have this law?

4. Write a paragraph to explain how you think our ancestors changed their way of life when they started making gardens.

5. What evidence is there to suggest that Papua New Guinea could indeed be one of the birthplaces of agriculture.

6. Draw a sketch map to show the location of Kuk plantation.

7. Trade

Trade is a very important activity of people. Evidence of trade gives us information about Man's settlement of an area. The oldest evidence of trade (i.e. the movement of goods from one area to another) in mainland New Guinea dates back 9000 years.

Date:	9000 years ago.
Place:	Kafiavana rock shelter, Eastern Highlands.
Evidence:	Remains of four shells.
Importance:	Signs of first real trade with the coast.

This site is 90 kilometres in a straight line from the north coast. Shells have been highly valued by the Highlanders and were traded for items such as stone.

Trading with Stone

People trade things they have for those they want. Stone from the Highlands has been found on both the north and south coasts. Finished stone axes and blades of high quality were made, and then traded over hundreds of kilometres. For a long time, axe heads were the main export from the Highlands valleys. It is thought that the whole population of Papua New Guinea were using stone axes which came from only a few main centres.

These men are collecting stone from a traditional quarry.

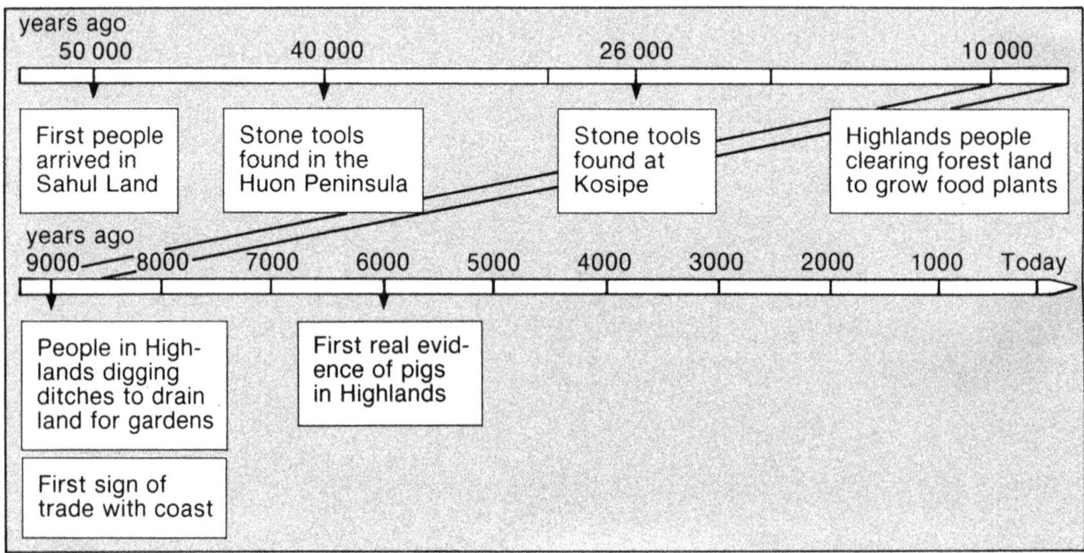

This man is making a stone axe.

Stone from the coast has also been traded to the Highlands. A black shiny stone, called **obsidian**, is mined in only three locations in Papua New Guinea; Fergusson Island in the Milne Bay Province, Lou Island in Manus Province, and Talasea in West New Britain Province.

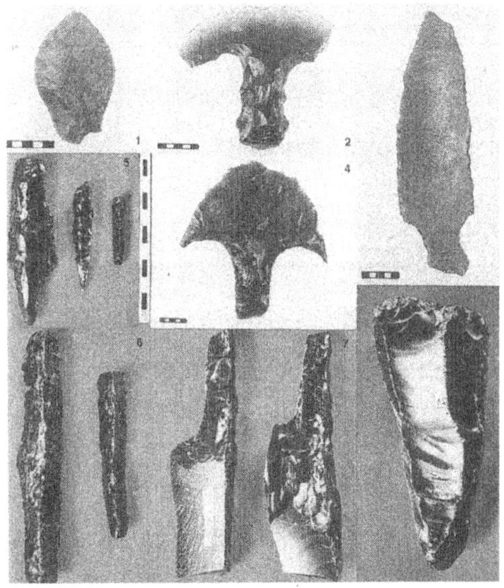

Obsidian tools.

It is a very highly valued stone because it can be made very sharp. There is evidence of obsidian being mined and traded throughout New Ireland 6000 years ago.

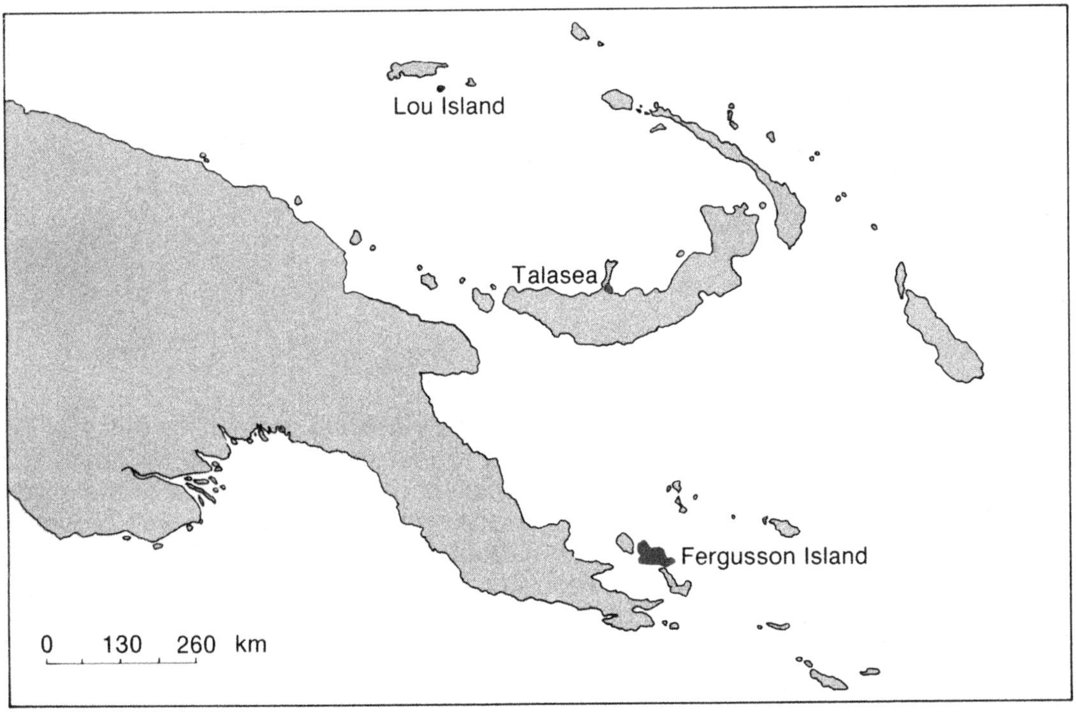

Lou Island
Talasea
Fergusson Island
0 130 260 km

Map showing where obsidian was mined.

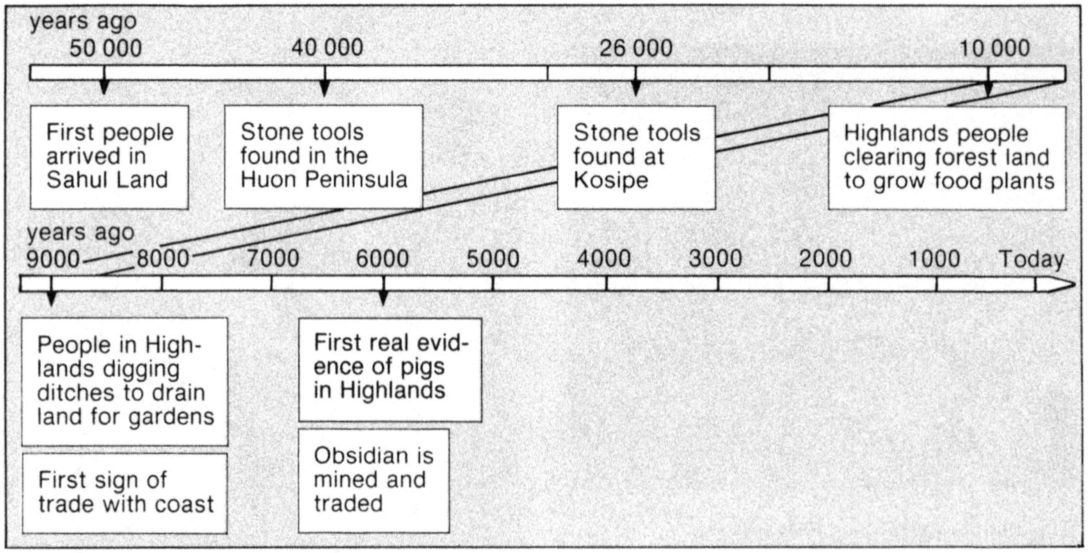

Obsidian remained a greatly valued and widely traded material until iron and glass became available.

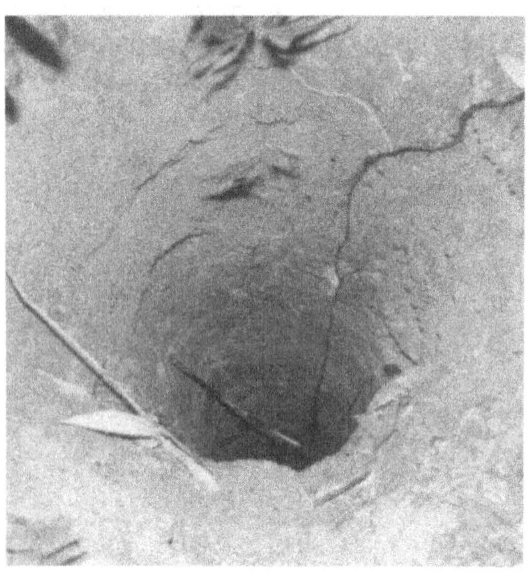

An obsidian mine.

Trading in stone and shell continued until the coming of Europeans to our country. Then, in the space of a very few years, this trade was almost destroyed. The stone axe trade was the first to go, killed by import of steel axes. Occasionally you may still find a stone axe being used by a craftsman.

A new trading partner for this tool is the tourist who is looking for anything which is old and rare. Most of the shell trade has now gone. This was brought about by new trade goods and cash, and by Europeans bringing in millions of shells, which destroyed their value. The shell trade survives only where shells are still used for important ceremonial occasions.

These shells are for a brideprice payment.

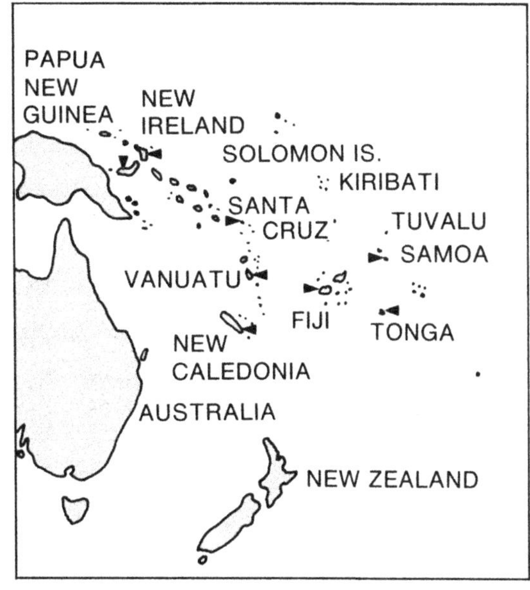

This map shows where Lapita pottery has been found.

Trading with Pots

Evidence of trading increases as we come nearer to the present time.

Date: 2000 years ago.
Place: Coastal and island Papua New Guinea; Watom Island, near Rabaul, East New Britain Province; Nebira, Yule Island and Oposisi in Central Province.
Evidence: Pottery.
Importance: Pottery trade well established. Oldest pottery in Papua New Guinea found at Watom Island. Similar pottery found in other parts of the Pacific.

Date: 1200 years ago.
Place: Wanigela, Northern Province.
Evidence: Pottery.
Importance: Similar pottery found in the Philippines.

Some of the oldest pottery found so far in Papua New Guinea comes from Watom Island, near Rabaul in East New Britain Province. Similar pottery has been found in parts of the Pacific. This pottery has been given the name **Lapita pottery**, after the place where it was first discovered, in New Caledonia.

Lapita pottery.

The people who made this type of pottery were obviously highly experienced long-distance sailors, since their pottery was so widely distributed. Many Lapita pottery sites have also produced small amounts of obsidian. This gives further proof of trading links. Lapita pottery dates from about 3500 years ago, and appears to have died out about 2000 years ago. The Papuan coast has produced evidence of pottery which is similar to the Lapita pottery. This could mean that the people from the Papuan coast traded with the people who made Lapita pottery.

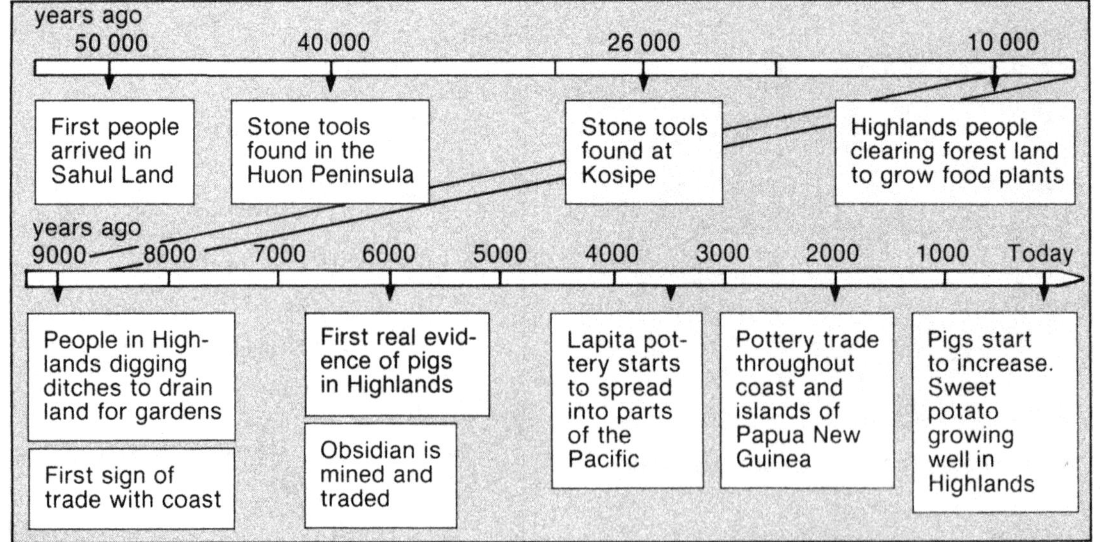

On the north-east coast at Wanigela, and in the Milne Bay Province, there is evidence of pottery being traded for other goods. The Kula Ring expeditions give evidence of this. You probably know about the recent (i.e. within living memory) Hiri trading expeditions in which the Motu people made yearly voyages to the Papuan Gulf. The Motuans exchanged their clay pots for sago and new hulls for their lakatois.

One of the lakatois from the Hiri Expedition.

This voyage no longer takes place today. The Motuans get the extra food they require by going to the trade store; they do not need new timber for building more lakatois. The Gulf people no longer need clay pots; they can buy their pots and pans from the store.

Some scientists, called linguists, have made a study of the languages of the Pacific region to see if there is any link between the different groups of people. These linguists have divided the many languages of Papua New Guinea into two main groups; **Austronesian** and **non-Austronesian**. The majority of Papua New Guinean languages belong to the non-Austronesian group. It is believed that these languages may have descended from the original language of the first settlers who arrived from Sunda Land about 50 000 years ago.

The linguists tell us that, although the language within the Austronesian group are very different in some ways, they are also very similar in others. They believe that the Austronesian language descended from a language which existed about 6000 years ago in south-east Asia.

The map below shows where these languages are spoken today.

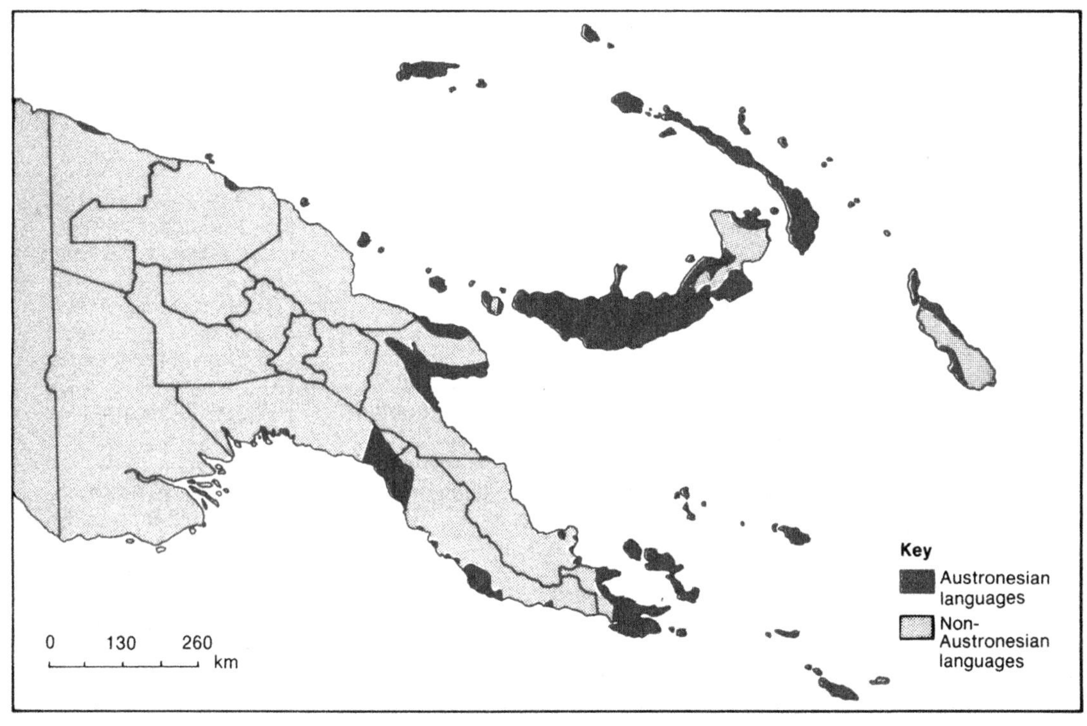

Map showing distribution of Austronesian and non-Austronesian languages.

If this is true, it is evidence for a second major migration of people from south-east Asia to the island of New Guinea and on into the Pacific. This migration would have taken place about 6000 years ago. Scientists still do not know. They are continuing their investigation of the evidence.

The chart on the following page is a summary of the major archaeological evidence of Man's presence in our island land mass.

Summary of Archaeological Evidence

DATE	PLACE	EVIDENCE	IMPORTANCE
40 000 years ago	Upper Swan River, Western Australia.	Stone tools.	People living in this corner of Australia probably came from south-east Asia about 53 000 years ago.
40 000 years ago	Huon Peninsula, Morobe Province.	Over 50 complete stone axes, and many broken ones.	One of these axes may be the oldest hafted stone axe in the world.
26 000 years ago	Kosipe, Central Province.	Stone axes and cutting tools.	Tools may have been used to assist in early gardening techniques.
12 000 years ago	Wanlek, Madang Province.	Evidence of human activity.	People living a settled life.
11 000 years ago	Kafiavana rock shelter, Eastern Highlands Province.	Stone axes and cutting tools.	These tools more developed than earlier tools. More suitable for clearing forest.
10 000 years ago	Kiowa and Niobe rock shelters, Eastern Highlands Province.	Stone tools, pigs' teeth.	Possible first signs of pigs. Perhaps a link with the coast.
	Yuku rock shelter, Western Highlands Province.	Stone tools, pigs' teeth.	
9000 years ago	Kafiavana rock shelter, Eastern Highlands Province.	Remains of shells.	First real evidence of trade with the coast.
9000 years ago	Kuk plantation, Western Highlands Province.	Remains of organic matter in man-made ditches.	Land used for growing food. Ditches draining land.
6000 years ago		More man-made ditches.	
2500–450 years ago		Digging sticks, stone axes.	Land abandoned. Gardens moved to hills.
6000 years ago	Balof rock shelter, New Ireland Province.	Pottery, pig bones, stone tools, obsidian stone.	People hunting and fishing, and probably gardening. Obsidian transported from Talasea, West New Britain Province.
? (not dated)	Kandrian, West New Britain Province.	Stone tools.	Several thousand years old.

DATE	PLACE	EVIDENCE	IMPORTANCE
5000 years ago	Kafiavana and Yuku rock shelters, Eastern Highlands Province; and Kiowa rock shelter, Western Highlands Province.	Pig and other animal bones; evidence of human activity.	Number of pigs starts to increase from now onwards.
2000 years ago	Coastal and island Papua New Guinea.	Abandoned settle-ments, burial sites, pottery.	Pottery trade well established.
	Watom Island, near Rabaul, East New Britain Province.	Pottery.	Oldest pottery found in Papua New Guinea. Similar pottery found in other parts of the Pacific.
	Nebira, Yulė Island and Oposisi, Central Province.	Animal and shell material, pottery and stone.	Gardening, hunting, fishing and trading. Pottery similar to Watom Island, near Rabaul.
2000 to 1600 years ago	Lake Birip and Lake Inim, near Mt Hagen, Western Highlands Province.	Plant evidence.	Many food gardens growing yams, taro, sugar-cane, bananas and beans.
1200 years ago	Wanigela, Northern Province.	Shell material, rubbish mound, pottery.	Similar pottery found in the Philippines.
400 years ago	Highlands region.	Sweet potato.	Slowly replaced taro as the main food crop.
Very recent	Whole of Papua New Guinea.	Introduction of many new animals and crops.	Major new influences.

You may be wondering how scientists manage to build up a picture about the life of our ancestors from all these separate pieces of evidence. In chapter 2 you learned a little bit about their work. As well as all the digging, finding, and recording, scientists must do a lot of thinking. Sometimes, they simply have to make a sensible guess based on the available evidence. As more evidence becomes available, scientists may find they have to change their minds about their first thoughts.

4. Copy and complete the following crossword in your exercise book.

Clues

Across

1 Old drainage ditches found in the highlands of Papua New Guinea.

9 Probably arrived in Sahul Land about 50 000 years ago.

10 The time before things were written down.

13 Study of ancient things.

16 This strait formed a land bridge between island New Guinea and Australia.

17 Diagram showing important events in history.

18 Same as 9 across.

19 Grown in gardens.

20 Remains have provided important archaeological evidence.

Down

2 Stone tools found here are 26 000 years old.

3 First people to arrive in island New Guinea came from south-east ______.

4 When the Earth's climate was much colder than today the sea levels were much ______ than at present.

5 Hafted stone axe found here may be the oldest in the world.

6 Major language group, found mainly in the coastal areas.

7 A staple food in many parts of Papua New Guinea; one type may have originated here.

8 This pottery dates from about 3500 years ago.

11 Scientific study of language.

12 Used by archaeologists to gather information about vegetation that existed in the past.

14 Can give valuable clues about life in the past.

15 A story about something which may have happened in the past.

Glossary

WORD	PAGE	MEANING
adapt	25	The way things change to suit new conditions.
ancestors	17	Those people one is descended from.
archaeologists	11	Scientists who study the things Man has made and used in the past.
artefact) artifact)	12	An object made or used by Man in the past.
astronomers	14	Scientists who study the stars.
Austronesian language	48	A group of languages found in coastal areas of Papua New Guinea and in other Pacific Islands.
biologists	14	Scientists who study living things and their remains.
climate	18	The pattern of temperature and rainfall over a long period of time.
earthquakes	6	A sudden movement of the Earth's surface.
evolution	25	The way that man, animals and plants have developed from simpler living things over millions of years.
fossils	10	The remains of a plant or animal changed into rock.
geologists	14	Scientists who study rocks.
hafted stone axe	29	An axe attached to a handle.
land bridge	19	The area of land between one place and another.
Lapita pottery	47	A type of pottery with a special design, which dates from 3500 to 2000 years ago.
linguists	13	Scientists who study different languages.
Man	7	Human beings.
marsupials	24	Animals which carry their young in a pouch.

monotremes	24	Animals with one body cavity for reproduction and excretion.
non-Austronesian language	48	Languages within our region not related to Austronesian languages.
obsidian	45	A dark volcanic glass-like stone.
origins	1	Starting points.
pollen	37	The fine powder formed on flowers, which fertilizes other flowers.
prehistory	10	The time before things were written down.
radio-carbon dating	13	A method for measuring the age of materials which contain carbon.
rodents	24	Animals such as rats and mice.
Sahul Land	19	The extended continent of Australia and island New Guinea.
solar system	4	The sun and the planets that circle around it.
Sunda Land	19	The extended continent of south-east Asia.
theory of evolution	25	Living things survive and multiply if they can adapt to their changing environment.
volcanic eruptions	6	Hot liquid rock forced up through the surface of the Earth.

Index